How Things Are Made

Berries to Jelly

By Inez Snyder

Welcome Books™

Children's Press®
A Division of Scholastic Inc.
New York / Toronto / London / Auckland / Sydney
Mexico City / New Delhi / Hong Kong
Danbury, Connecticut

Photo Credits: Cover © StockFood/Brauner; p. 5 © StockFood/Arras; p. 7 © StockFood/ FoodPhotography Eising; pp. 9, 15 © StockFood/Mewes; pp. 11, 17, 19 © StockFood/Rees; p. 13 © StockFood/Eising; p. 21 © Denis Boissavy/Getty Images

Contributing Editor: Shira Laskin
Book Design: Christopher Logan

Library of Congress Cataloging-in-Publication Data

Snyder, Inez.
    Berries to jelly / by Inez Snyder.
    p. cm.—(How things are made)
    Includes index.
    ISBN 0-516-25196-1 (lib. bdg.)—ISBN 0-516-25526-6 (pbk.)
    1. Jelly—Juvenile literature. 2. Cookery (Berries)—Juvenile literature. I.Title. II. Series.

TX612.J4S58 2005
641.8'52—dc22

                                                    2004010332

Contents

Jelly is made from **berries**.

The berries are cooked in a pot.

This makes the juice inside the berries come out.

The berries and juice are **strained** into another pot.

Only the juice is left.

Sugar is added to the juice.

Sugar will help make the jelly taste **sweet**.

The juice and the sugar are **stirred**.

The juice and the sugar cook until they are very hot.

They must **boil** to become jelly.

The jelly is done cooking.

It is poured into jars.

17

Lids are put on top of the jars.

Now the jelly must cool.

The jelly is finished.

Jelly tastes good!

New Words

berries (**ber**-eez) the seeds or fruits of plants that are often small and round, such as strawberries, raspberries, and blueberries

boil (**boil**) when water or other liquids get very hot and have bubbles on the surface

jelly (**jel**-ee) a sweet, sticky food that is made from fruit juice and sugar heated together until they become a thick and smooth mixture

lids (**lidz**) tops or covers

stirred (**stuhrd**) mixed by being moved around in a container with a spoon

strained (**straynd**) poured through a container with tiny holes to separate the solids from the liquid

sugar (**shug**-uhr) a white or brown food that comes from a plant and is used to make other foods sweet

sweet (**sweet**) having the taste of sugar or honey

To Find Out More

Books
From Fruit to Jelly
by Shannon Zemlicka
Lerner Publishing Group

The Berry Book
by Gail Gibbons
Holiday House, Inc.

Web Site
All Recipes Index: Jams and Jellies
http://www.allrecipes.com/directory/2698.asp
Search this Web site to learn how to make different kinds of
jelly with an adult.

Index

About the Author
Inez Snyder writes books to help children learn how to read.

Content Consultant
Jason Farrey, The Culinary Institute

Reading Consultants
Kris Flynn, Coordinator, Small School District Literacy, The San Diego County
    Office of Education

Shelly Forys, Certified Reading Recovery Specialist, W.J. Zahnow Elementary
    School, Waterloo, IL

Paulette Mansell, Certified Reading Recovery Specialist, and Early Literacy
    Consultant, TX